Receiving God's Love
The Practice of
Radical Hospitality

Robert Schnase

ABINGDON PRESS
Nashville

Receiving God's Love:
The Practice of Radical Hospitality

All rights reserved.

Originally appeared in *Five Practices of Fruitful Living* by Robert Schnase,
which was published by Abingdon Press in 2010.

ISBN 978-1-6308-8298-3

14 15 16 17 18 19 20 21 22 23--10 9 8 7 6 5 4 3 2 1
MANUFACTURED IN THE UNITED STATES OF AMERICA

Contents

Receiving God's Love
The Practice of
Radical Hospitality

Listen! I am standing at the door, knocking; if you hear my voice and open the door, I will come in to you and eat with you, and you with me.
—*Revelation 3:20*

The Fruitful Living Series

Jesus taught a way of life and invited people into a relationship with God that was vibrant, dynamic and fruitful. He said, "I am the vine, you are the branches. Those who abide in me and I in them bear much fruit... My father is glorified by this, that you bear much fruit and become my disciples," (John 15: 5, 8). Jesus wanted people to flourish.

Scripture is sprinkled with phrases that point to fruitful living—the kingdom of God, eternal life, immeasurable riches, a peace that passes all understanding, abundant life.

How do I cultivate a life that is abundant, fruitful, purposeful, and deep? What are the commitments, critical risks, and practices that open me to God's transforming grace and that help me discover the difference God intends for me to make in the world?

How do I live the fruitful, flourishing life of a follower of Christ?

Radical Hospitality. Passionate Worship. Intentional Faith Development. Risk-Taking Mission and Service. Extravagant Generosity.

Since the publication of *Five Practices of Fruitful Congregations,* these edgy, provocative, dangerous words have helped hundreds of congregations understand their mission, renew ministries, and stretch toward fruitfulness and excellence for the purposes of Christ.

The Fruitful Living Series moves the discussion of Christian practice from the congregational level to the personal practices of discipleship. The fruitful God-related life develops with intentional and repeated attention to five essential practices that are critical for our growth in Christ.

Radical Hospitality in our personal walk with Christ begins with an extraordinary receptivity to the grace of God. In distinctive and personal ways, we invite God into our hearts and make space for God in our lives. We receive God's love and offer it to others.

Through the practice of *Passionate Worship*, we learn to love God in return. We practice listening to God, allowing God to shape our hearts and minds through prayer, personal devotion, and community worship. We love God.

Through the practice of *Intentional Faith Development*, we do the soul work that connects us to others, immerses us in God's word, and positions us to grow in grace and mature in Christ. We learn in community.

The practice of *Risk-Taking Mission and Service* involves offering ourselves in purposeful service to others in need,

making a positive difference even at significant personal cost and inconvenience to our own lives. We serve.

Through the practice of *Extravagant Generosity*, we offer our material resources in a manner that supports the causes that transform life and relieve suffering and that enlarges the soul and sustains the spirit. We give back.

These five practices - to receive God's love, to love God in return, to grow in Christ, to serve others, and to give back—are so essential to growth in Christ and to the deepening of the spiritual life that failure to attend to them, develop them, and deepen them with intentionality limits our capacity to live fruitfully and fully, to settle ourselves completely in God, and to become instruments of God's transforming grace. The adjectives—*radical, passionate, intentional, risk-taking,* and *extravagant*—provoke us out of complacency and remind us that these practices require more than haphazard, infrequent, and mediocre attention.

These practices open our heart—to God, to others, to a life that matters, a life rich with meaning, relationship, and contribution. They help us flourish.

Christian Practice

The ministry of Jesus is grounded in personal practices. Jesus' life is marked by prayer, solitude, worship, reflection, the study of scripture, conversation, community, serving, engagement with suffering, and generosity. These personal practices sustained a ministry that opened people to God's grace, transformed human hearts, and changed the circumstances of people in need.

Christian practices are those essential activities we repeat and deepen over time. They create openings for God's spirit to shape us. Practices are not simply principles we talk about; practices are something we do. They make our faith a tangible and visible part of daily life. We see them

done in the life of Jesus, and we do them until they become a way of life for us. We become instruments of God's grace and love.

Through practice, we open ourselves to grace and let ourselves be opened by grace. We follow Christ, step by step, day by day, again and again; and by these steps and through these days, we are changed, we become someone different, we become new creations in Christ.

The books in this series are based on the premise that by repeating and deepening certain fundamental practices, we cooperate with God in our own growth in Christ and participate with the Holy Spirit in our own spiritual maturation. The fundamental practices are rooted in scripture and derived from the clear imperatives of the life of Christ. This isn't a self-improvement, pull-yourself-up-by-your-own-bootstraps notion of how we grow in grace. It's not about trying harder, working longer, or striving more to achieve God's blessing.

The Christian life is a gift of God, an expression of God's grace in Christ, the result of an undeserved and unmerited offering of love toward us. Every step of the journey toward Christ is preceded by, made possible by, and sustained by the perfecting grace of God.

The fruitful life is cultivated by placing ourselves in the most advantageous places to see, receive, learn, and understand the love that has been offered in Christ.

How to Use *The Fruitful Living Series*

The Fruitful Living Series is deeply personal, and as such it is composed of stories—the experiences, hopes, doubts, good efforts, and false starts of people like you and me. Faith journeys are used to illustrate key points so as to encourage honest reflection and conversation. But the approach is not individualistic—only about me, my, and mine. Every experience imbeds us more deeply in the community of Christ because it is in the presence of our sisters and brothers that our spirits are sustained, our hearts encouraged.

I pray for those who reach for these books searching for understanding about their own faith journeys, that it may stimulate them to deeper life in Christ. But I pray especially for those who have been handed these books and who open their pages reluctantly, that they may open themselves to the possibility that something in the stories and reflections

may cause them to think more deeply, pray more earnestly, and serve others in a more fruitful and satisfying way.

This series is experiential rather than systematic or dogmatic. It relies on the experiences of ordinary people who have been extraordinarily shaped by their relationship to God. None of us has the complete picture. Movement toward Christ is never a straight line, uninterrupted, obstacle free, totally consistent, predictable, and easily describable. There are no perfect accounts that capture everything that lies behind and no completely reliable maps that outline the future in one's faith journey. Soul work is hard, and following Christ is messy, challenging, joyous, scary, painful, sustaining, and frustratingly indescribable.

This *Fruitful Living Series* is about the everyday faith of everyday people seeking to listen for God, to love each other, to care for those in need, to embrace the stranger, to live the fruit of the spirit.

These books are practical. They are about what we do daily and intentionally, and about who we become because of how God uses what we do. They suggest a compass rather than map; a direction helpful for many diverse contexts rather than a specific step-by-step, how-to plan that fits only certain terrain.

Engage the material personally. Discover what you can learn about yourself, your relationship with God, your personal desires and internal resistances in the life of faith.

And read *The Fruitful Living Series* with others on the journey to Christ. Use it in house groups, adult Sunday school classes, a weeknight book study, or with your family. Resolve to deepen your own practices of faith. Pray for one another and support one another in Christ. Encourage church leaders and pastors to use the book in retreats, sermon series, or evening studies. These books focus the essential work that forms disciples; by cultivating these practices in the lives of those reached by the community

of faith, the congregation fulfills its mission of making disciples of Jesus Christ for the transformation of the world.

As a pastor and bishop, I've been granted the privilege of witnessing people whose faith is immeasurably greater than my own, whose sacrifice more than I myself could ever bear, whose impact in the lives of others through their service is immeasurably more than mine, whose personal discipline, depth of spirit, and maturing in Christ is far ahead of anything I shall ever achieve or hope to receive, and whose generosity is so extraordinary that it humbles me completely. This book is about how we learn from their fruitfulness in Christ so that we cooperate with God in becoming what God created us to be.

My prayer for you and your congregation is that this series helps us all grow in grace and in the knowledge and love of God. May we be changed from the inside out so that we can transform the world for the purposes of Christ.

STRUCK BY GRACE:
You Are Loved

> *We love because he first loved us.*
> *—1 John 4:19*

"Accept that you are accepted." When I read this as a college student, those words by Paul Tillich jolted me into a new understanding of God's unconditional love.1 The pivotal first element in our walk of faith—the practice of Radical Hospitality—involves our saying Yes to God's love for us, a willingness to open our lives to God and invite God into our hearts. It involves our capacity to receive grace, accept Christ's love, and make room for God in our lives.

"Do we know what it means to be struck by grace?" Tillich asks. This was a provocative notion to me, an odd metaphor, to describe God's grace as something that strikes, that jars us into a new way of thinking, that collides with our old way of being. He continues, "We cannot transform our lives, unless we allow them to be transformed by that stroke of grace." The first movement toward the new creation, the transformed life, and becoming the person God wants us to be begins when we face the startling reality of God's unconditional love for us. Receiving the

love and forgiveness of God, beginning to comprehend its meaning, and opening ourselves to the new life it brings can be as disrupting as an earthquake, as abrupt as lightening striking across the black night sky. It means we've been struck by grace.

The personal practice of Radical Hospitality begins with a receiving, perceiving, listening, opening, accepting attitude—a readiness to accept and welcome God's initiative toward us. It is sustained with active behaviors that place us in the most advantageous posture to continue to receive God, welcome Christ, and make room for grace. And so it involves interior decision and soul work, a listening and receptivity to God, as well as habits that transform us as we regularly, frequently, and intentionally make room in our lives for God.

Grace strikes at unexpected times, Tillich suggests: when we are in pain, feeling restless, empty, alone, estranged, or when we feel disgust, weakness, or hostility. It strikes us when other things don't work, when we feel directionless and useless, when compulsions reign, and darkness overshadows. When the ordinariness of life grinds us down, or the vacuity of the world's promises leaves us empty, when we finally realize our churning and churning is taking us nowhere fast, in such moments, grace comes to us like a wave of light in the darkness, and we perceive a voice saying, "You are accepted."

"We don't know the name of it at the time; there will be much to learn later," Tillich writes. We don't have to promise anything at the time, for in that moment we are fundamentally the recipients of a promise. We don't have to give anything; only to receive what is given. Our only and singular task is to *accept* that we are accepted.

You are *loved*. You *are* loved. *You* are loved. Can you accept that?

God's love for us is not something we have to strive for, earn, work on, or fear. It is freely given. That is key: that we are loved, first, finally, and forever by God, a love so deep and profound and significant that God offers his Son to signify and solidify this love forever so that we get it.

The journey to becoming what God would have us to be begins with opening ourselves to this love, and giving it a place in our hearts. The journey begins when the God "up there" or "out there," the God whom we perceive as some philosophical abstraction, becomes a living truth and a love that we receive into ourselves. The welcoming requires of us an extraordinary hospitality, a radical receptivity, a willingness to allow God to come in and dwell within our hearts.

I first read Tillich's essay while sitting on grass near a fountain outside a campus library on a bright spring morning. I'd been active in church for years and was contemplating the call to ministry. I was rethinking the faith of my childhood and struggling with the normal things college students wrestle with. I was more clear about what I did not believe than about what I did believe. A student group at church was reading Tillich, a well-known theologian, and I was doing my assignment.

Tillich described those things that separate us from God and one another. He wrote about feeling unaccepted and about striving to prove, earn, justify, or validate ourselves. This resonated deeply with the feelings of uncertainty, pain, and struggle that I experienced as a student wrestling with the expectations of parents, the pressure of peers, the yearning to fit in, the desire to make a difference. His words somehow stimulated a rush of thoughts about life's meaning, connection, and direction. I kept looking up from the text to the fountain, lost in my own thoughts, yet soothed by whispers of flowing water. The Spirit was breaking through, stirring my soul, and moving me to deeper places.

Accept that you are accepted. In the moment that grace strikes, grace conquers sin. Lingering guilt that has grown tumor-like for years in the dark recesses of a person's soul can lose its deathly power. Grace helps us face the truth about ourselves, to embrace it rather than run from it; and by embracing this truth and offering it to God, we discover that God knows the truth about us and still loves us, and that God will shape us from this day forward anew. God's been waiting for us, desiring us to let him in. Can we accept that we are accepted?

Grace, when we really absorb its full meaning and consequence, causes us to rethink the direction and momentum of our lives, to change course, to break through the pretense and pride and see ourselves as we really are—utterly and completely unable by our own striving and effort to make it all work. The love of God pierces the veneer, breaks through the resistances, pulls us out of ourselves, and takes us into the deepest of mysteries of the spiritual life. Our worth is grounded in God's grace.

JUST SAY YES!

Richard wanted to know what we are supposed to say *Yes* to when he first saw the tagline "Say *Yes*!" on all the bulletins, banners, and websites of First United Methodist Church of Sedalia, Missouri. As he began to explore the spiritual life through worship, prayer, Bible study, and service, he realized that every single step in following Christ involves saying *Yes* . . . yes to God, yes to the spiritual life, yes to serving, yes to giving, yes to life.

At what points have you said Yes to God when you could have said *No*, and saying *Yes* has made all the difference?

When we finally get it, and open our hearts to the truth of God's love for us, we begin to receive glimpses of a peace that the world cannot give or take away, an inner assurance about our ultimate worth in God's eyes that surpasses understanding.

God creates us. God loves us. God desires a relationship with us. In the revealing moment, our singular task is not to harden our hearts but to open them to God, to open our lives to grace, to receive, and to say *Yes*. Radical Hospitality begins by welcoming God in rather than slamming the door closed.

Have you ever been struck by grace?

Reading those words by Tillich more than thirty years ago, I could see so many of the events of my faith journey with greater clarity, the initiative of God's grace reaching out to me through the lives of many people. God has wanted in.

I experienced the feeling of life beginning anew, taking hold. In that moment, the rest of my life was given to me as a gift.

Accept that you are accepted. Open the doors of your heart.

A Look at Grace

Can you remember one moment in your life that changed all the others? Have you experienced an event that caused the ground to shift beneath you? Have you ever experienced the unexpected and irreversible unraveling of all the previous understandings of yourself and your world? What has been the most overwhelming and determining experience of your life? A love? A loss? A birth? A truth?

Accepting that you are accepted can be such a moment. Being struck by grace can prove such a time. Inviting God in alters everything. Love changes us, and through us, it changes others around us.

Scripture tells many stories of unexpected grace. Saul on the Damascus road, Zacchaeus, Mary Magdalene, the woman beside the well, the worshipful Mary and her obsessive sister Martha, the man paralyzed beside the pool, the woman accused of adultery, the soldier with a dying son, the thief on the cross—what happened to them all? Struck by grace each and every one, penetrated by the unfathomable and overwhelming truth of God's love for them, their self-images shattered and replaced with a whole new way of seeing themselves and the world, their old ways broken by an amazing grace. In both ordinary and radical ways, they opened their hearts to God and invited God in.

Through Jesus, God said *Yes* to them, and each in her or his own way found the courage to say *Yes* to God; and in that interchange, all things became new. God's welcoming of them was met with a new hospitality toward God.

God's love has a piercing quality, a persevering element, an assertive and searching aspect. God yearns for us, woos us, reaches for us. God's grace has the generative power to pardon, transform, redeem, and perfect, and it pushes and pursues. God's love is not something sitting on a shelf that we reach for, but a truth at the heart of life that reaches for us. God's grace interrupts with a compelling, propelling, motivating, and mobilizing quality. It has the power, if we let it, to break open our hearts, get inside of us, change us, and then work its way through us to others.

The experience and insight of countless of our forebears for hundreds of years is that when we delve deeply into the

THE MYSTERY OF GRACE

"I do not at all understand the mystery of grace—only that it meets us where we are but does not leave us where it found us."[2]
—Anne Lamott

interior life and begin the spiritual journey, we seek what is true and good only to discover that something is seeking us; that in our yearning, something longs for us; in our desire to know, we find ourselves known. It's not that we love first, but that we are first loved. This active, reaching quality of God's love is what grace refers to, a gift-like initiative on God's part toward us. On the Sistine Chapel ceiling, Michelangelo's famous painting depicts humanity reaching for God only to discover God reaching all the more toward us.

God loves you. Period.

And the first critical step in the journey of faith involves a *Radical Hospitality*, our opening our hearts to God's love, letting God into our lives to work with us.

Every person we admire, respect, and desire to emulate for their spirituality, wisdom, graciousness, service, and generosity at some point explicitly and dramatically,

or unknowingly and gradually, decided to let God in. They said *Yes* to God's love and opened the door to allow God in. They didn't have all their beliefs figured out, and maybe they still don't, but in their pattern of receiving, God stopped being merely an idea and became personal for them, a part of them, an element of their daily lives, a resident in their heart.

They accepted God's acceptance of them, and allowed this truth to shape and change them, dramatically and quickly in some and gradually in others.

Paul writes, "For by *grace* you have been *saved* through *faith*, and this is not your own doing; it is the gift of God" (Ephesians 2:8, emphasis added). *Saved* means that we come into a right relationship with God, becoming what God created us to be. *Saved* refers to our becoming whole, our living fully and abundantly the fruitful life. Paul says there are two essential and operative elements to this whole and right relationship with God, *grace* and *faith.*

Grace refers to the gift-like quality of God's love, the initiating power and presence of God in our lives. *Grace* is God accepting us, despite our rejecting or ignoring or rebelling against God's love.

Grace is God offering us a relationship, loving us. It is the unexpected UPS package delivered to our front door with our name on it.

Faith is our acceptance of the gift, the opening of our hearts to invite God's love into our lives. *Faith* is our receiving God's grace, love, and pardon, and allowing these gifts to shape us and make us anew. *Faith* is the commitment again and again to live by grace, to honor the gift, and use it, and pass it along. *Faith* is accepting the UPS package, signing on the dotted line, taking it inside our house, unwrapping it, and discovering its treasure.

God's gracious love for us, and the capacity for that love to change our lives when we open ourselves to it, and through us to change the world—this is the central

story of the Christian journey. "For God so loved the world that he gave his only Son, so that everyone who believes in him may not perish but may have eternal life" (John 3:16). This verse, the "Gospel in Miniature," captures the interchange between grace and faith and the new life it brings.

Jesus is the ultimate expression of God's grace, God becoming human in order to reach us and to make possible living abundantly, meaningfully, lovingly, and gracefully.

Frequently, we view God as some cosmic entity existing beyond our experience, removed from daily life, an abstraction of the mind. But the God we see revealed in Jesus Christ is not some passive general benevolence that leaves things alone. The God we see revealed in Jesus is the God of *grace*, an active, searching, embracing, assertive love. It is a strong, persevering, gritty grace that gives Jesus the power to embrace untouchable lepers, sit with outcast tax collectors, visit with forbidden strangers. The grace

of the Lord Jesus Christ is the steel courage to intercede against the violence and injustice of angry authorities on behalf of a woman accused of adultery. It is an earthy, practical grace that causes Jesus to kneel before his friends, take a towel from his waist, and wash their feet, daring them to do likewise as a way of life. It is an unrelenting and irresistible grace that never gives up on either the hopeless and despairing or the rich and powerful. It is the disturbing, interruptive grace that overturns the tables of the cheating money changer in the temple. It is the perceptive, affirming grace that notices the widow with her two coins, a soldier mourning the death of his son, a farmer pruning vines. It is the compassionate grace that embraces the victims of violence and the persistent grace that steps into cellblocks with prisoners. It is the challenging, correcting, indicting grace that confronts unjust judges, self-justifying lawyers, unsympathetic rich people, and haughty religious leaders. It is the costly, sacrificial grace that dares to absorb the violence of humiliation, unjust persecution, and torturous death to reveal the depth of God's love for humanity.

The love of God revealed in Jesus extends to the outcast and the insider, the despairing and the self-satisfied, to the religious as well as to those who actively or indifferently reject faith.

Jesus not only loved people no one else loved, but his grace also extended to the unlovable and hidden parts of those who lived otherwise good and faithful lives. By washing the feet of his disciples, Jesus symbolically touched the dirtiest, most offensive part of each person's life, demonstrating an unexpected love. *Grace* is God's loving activity embracing our lostness, brokenness, hurt, and rebellion, so that we may experience forgiveness, reconciliation, and liberation, which come only through our receiving this love into our lives. A radical encounter with the grace of God may not solve everything overnight, but many things remain beyond our ability to solve until we at least take the first step of accepting the grace of God and inviting God's love in.

The piercing quality of God's love disrupts people. It does not leave us alone and will not let us go. This love breaks through pretense, shatters previous self-understandings, reshapes priorities, turns the world upside down. Being struck by grace is not simply adopting a new attitude, feeling better about ourselves, changing our image, or giving ourselves a lift. The result of Radical Hospitality, a cultivated receptivity to God's grace, causes people who are going down one path to change direction and take another instead.

John Wesley, the founder of Methodism, discovered that even he himself could be unexpectedly struck anew by God's grace. He records in his journal a moment when the reality of God's grace pierced his heart, changing him again forever. "In the evening I went very unwillingly to a society in Aldersgate Street, where one was reading Luther's preface to the Epistle to the Romans. About a quarter before nine, while he was describing the change which God works in the heart through faith in Christ, I felt my heart

strangely warmed. I felt I did trust in Christ, in Christ alone for salvation; And an assurance was given me, that he had taken away *my* sins, even *mine*, and saved *me* from the law of sin and death."[3]

Accept that you are accepted. The most important journey you will ever take begins by saying *Yes*, by receiving God's love and accepting God's acceptance of you. With lives filtered through a promise, the followers of Jesus live sustained by the assurance of God's unending love. A continuing receptivity to God's initiative in our lives is the key to all the practices that lead to fruitful living.

REFLECTION

"LISTEN! *I am standing at the door*, KNOCKING; *if you hear* MY VOICE *and open the door*, I WILL *come in to you and eat with* YOU, *and* YOU *with* ME."

—*Revelation 3:20*

God's love for us is not something we have to strive for, earn, work on, or fear. It is freely given.
That is key: that we are loved, first, finally, and forever by God.

Questions

- When have you experienced a time in your life when unexpected love changed you? How did it change you?

- How have you felt God's unconditional love? Has it shaped your desire to do personal soul work?

- How do you understand the phrase "struck by grace"?

- Through what persons or events have you experienced the initiating, searching quality of God's love? How did you let God in?

Prayer

Lord, open my eyes to the striking power of your grace at work in me and in the lives of those around me. Your unexpected love restores me and brings me back to myself.

OBSTACLES TO GRACE:
Distractions and Defenses

*Do not be conformed to this world,
but be transformed by the renewing of
your minds, so that you may discern
what is the will of God—what is good
and acceptable and perfect.
—Romans 12:2*

God loves you. This is the story of grace. If this is so, why is that so hard for us to hear and know this truth?

Ten thousand obstacles prevent our receiving God's love and make us inhospitable to God's initiative. We fail to open ourselves to God's love, even when we hear these words spoken to us because other voices are repeated even more frequently.

Cultural Voices

The voices of our commercial culture repeat themselves over and over, influencing us through television, radio, magazines, billboards, the Internet, iPods and iPhones; and all these voices penetrate our lives to influence our perceptions of ourselves. Like a magnet beside a compass that draws the needle away from its true bearing, these cultural voices make it hard for us to move in directions that are positive, that lead to peace and happiness, or that open us to the spiritual life. We have difficulty valuing things appropriately. These influences feed the myth that

our worth and happiness rest with what kind of car we drive or clothes we wear, or what kind of "look" we have or income we earn.

An interesting contradiction puzzles sociologists and psychologists. Since World War II, we've faced a time of unprecedented prosperity and material well-being in Western societies. No era in human history has ever been more richly blessed with progress in health, longevity, protection from the elements, speed of transportation and ease of communication, safety from illness and pandemic and famine, and security from the violence of war. We've had more liberty, more choices, more options, more mobility, and more freedom from fear than at any time in the history of the earth.[4]

So, why have we not been happier? Why have nearly all measures of contentedness, connection, and a sustaining sense of purpose declined? As we've developed the practical, technical, and material skills for living prosperously, the spiritual skills for living happily, wisely, generously, and meaningfully have weakened. Cultural voices replay the myth that a good life comes from the practice of buying, possessing, and accumulating, and this fosters a thin, elusive, transient, watery happiness. The thick, rich, lasting notion of a good life, of life abundant and fruitful, comes from deeper sources. It grows from the awareness that God loves us, and from the persistent soul work, the repeated opening of ourselves to God to let ourselves be changed, and from loving and being loved by others. This alone stands as the unassailable and intrinsic source of our living happily, peacefully, and fruitfully.

Fast-Forward Living

The rapid speed and intensity of our high-tech and highly mobile lifestyles distract us from fathoming the spiritual life and the depth of God's love for us. For many of us, every moment of our waking days is filled with movement, activity, and sound. Directed by our handheld planners

and connected by our computers and cell phones, we move in fast-forward from home to work and back again, to children's activities, sports events, entertainment venues, fast food restaurants. From the awakening alarm until the final "click" closing our Internet browsers, our lives are surrounded by sensations that keep us focused on the motion and movement of the physical world, immersed in tangible sounds and sights and the pressing immediacy of what's expected next from us.

The risk is a rather shallow and surface existence, investing enormous amounts of time, passion, and energy in many things that simply do not merit it—distractedly and purposelessly surfing the Net, noodling away time with computer games, flipping channels through an array of admittedly vacuous choices on television.

These are the cultural waters through which we swim daily, and life is too short not to spend some time in pure escape, unapologetically enjoying our leisure.

On the other hand, where does a pattern of twenty or thirty years of unrestrained and unreflective immersion in these distractions and entertainments take us? How do these form us? What kind of person do they help us become? Everything we do is a spiritual practice, building up or tearing down our spiritual fabric, deepening or ignoring life with God. Do our current patterns enrich our spirits and glorify God, or impoverish our inner life and avoid God?

Name one person you desire to model your life after because of what they consume, or because of all the television they watch, or celebrity details they know.

Intuitively, we know that this type of living does not lead to the rich-textured life that ultimately satisfies. We perceive the difference between living thinly and living deeply, fruitfully, and abundantly. Life lived entirely on the superficial level lacks depth, purpose, connection. It misses the sacred. It avoids the spiritual, and we are at greater

risk of this than we sometimes acknowledge. Distracted by television, the Internet, and iPods and focused on the recurring urgencies of making a living, maintaining our health, paying the bills, fulfilling our basic family obligations—there's hardly time or space to contemplate where all this is taking us. Like water bugs skimming dizzily in circles on the surface of a pool, we can live oblivious to the depth and height and expanse of existence.

Paul warns about this danger when he writes, "Do not be conformed to this world . . ." (Romans 12:2), or as one translation says, "Don't let the world . . . squeeze you into its own mold" (JBP).

The conscientious person trying to figure out how to flourish amidst the daily influences of the culture perceives an underlying question: How do I find God in this world in which I live? How do I allow God into my life? Those mentors and examples of fruitful living we admire have discovered what Paul calls the "indescribable gift" of

IT FITS ME BETTER

Gloria describes the sudden truth that occurred to her one day as she found herself cleaning up the beer cans the morning after a late night of channel surfing with her husband. The number of cans kept growing. "What kind of life is this? Where is this going?" she and her husband asked themselves. They decided to risk something different. They began to explore the spiritual life by attending a congregation. The whole environment was new to them, but they kept opening themselves to new experiences. They discovered others searching like themselves. Gradually, they found themselves shifting how they used their time, what they talked about, what activities they connected to. Five years later Gloria says, "We changed in ways we couldn't have imagined. My life as I live it now would be a total stranger to my former self. I'm becoming a different person, and it fits me better."

God's grace (2 Corinthians 9:15). They have opened themselves more deeply to the interior life, the life of soul and spirit, the path of the holy and sacred. They have made critical choices and developed patterns and practices of living that have helped them access life with God.

God is in the depth, and we lose touch with God when we focus only on surface things. God is in the silence, which we neglect and fear, and we close ourselves to the whisperings of the Spirit when we constantly surround ourselves with artificial sounds. God is in the questions that arise when we break free of the distractions, and we cut God off when we avoid contemplations of purpose, value, and priority. God is in the mystery, and we turn God away when we live as if the only things that matter are those we can see, touch, explain, or possess. God is in the love of others, and we drive God out when we neglect the deepening of relationships. God is in the feeling of being still, and we overlook attempts by God to reach us when we run constantly from one activity to another. God is in the discovery and exploration of the interior life, and we say *No* to God when we deny there is a spiritual side to our own lives. There are elements to existence that we only discover when we open ourselves to God.

The fast-forward focus on surface things contrasts with the lives our ancestors lived. Our great-grandparents spent long hours in repetitive tasks, usually with other members of their family or community, working with their hands, surrounded by the natural sounds of home, farm, kitchen, neighborhood, and community. Whether they worked the fields, hunted in the woods, labored in the workshop, or sweated in the kitchen, most had hours each day to think, remember, mull over, rehearse, and reflect on the happenings of their lives. The meaning of events filtered regularly through a thousand internal permutations and reconsiderations, tested and shaped by conversation and community. Their routines gave time for the mind and heart to contemplate and to connect to others.

Today, it's hard to develop the interior capacity to listen for God or the readiness of soul that makes room for God's grace. Distraction dulls us to the sharper truths. We lose something when we are too distracted; having no deep relationships changes us. Like passengers on a speeding train trying to hear the whispers of a stranger standing beside the tracks, the dizzying intensity, unrelenting forward motion, and insulation of our culture make it hard for us to really hear God's word and feel God's love. Hearing God requires deliberate soul work. Spirituality and speed do not go together well.

Fifty or sixty years of a life defined by doing what's next, responding to the expectations of others, shaped entirely by the urgencies of work and the voices of culture—that's the risk of superficial living. If we do not intentionally ask, "What am I here for?" and "Where am I going?" these cultural influences will propel us along the surface of life, forming an identity not of our own shaping and providing

a destination not of our own choosing. We can become what we never intended to be.

Unfortunately, even our religious involvements may contribute nothing but additional activity on the surface level of living if those involvements merely support the same values and goals that conform us to the world. Attending programs, meetings, and performances, we may find ourselves behaving outwardly religious while avoiding genuine explorations of the interior life. It's as easy to close the door to God's grace in our church life as it is in our life at home, work, or leisure. We can sing the choruses of how Jesus loves us while inwardly failing to make space in our souls for the truly transforming power of that love. Religion must do more than just help us fit in better and get ahead faster according to the world's values.

REFLECTION

"You shall **LOVE** *the* **LORD** *your* **GOD** *with all your* **HEART,** *and with all your* **SOUL,** *and with all your* **STRENGTH,** *and with all your* **MIND;** *and your* **NEIGHBOR** *as* **YOURSELF."**

—*Luke 10:27*

Do our current patterns enrich our spirits and glorify God, or impoverish our inner life and avoid God?

Questions

- How do you compare the inner happiness that comes from God's Spirit with the happiness defined by the culture?

- What personal values or practices help you cultivate the good life?

- Where do you experience silence in your life?

- How do you feel about silence? What about it refreshes and invigorates you? What do you learn from it?

Prayer

Forgive me, Lord, for the many ways I neglect you and shut you out, and for all that obscures your great hope and love for me and others. Find me once again, and bring me home to you.

OBSTACLES TO GRACE:
Internal Messages and Personal Choices

*So if anyone is in Christ,
there is a new creation: everything old
has passed away; see,
everything has become new!*
—2 Corinthians 5:17

In addition to external distractions, internal pressures also complicate receiving God's love—negative family voices that replay through our minds, distorting our ability to absorb the truth that God loves us. The struggles we've had to overcome in order to feel loved, accepted, respected, or appreciated limit our ability to receive God's love. Many of us still endlessly pursue the affirmation of a father or mother, even if they are deceased, or we strive to win the approval of a significant teacher, coach, or mentor whose disapproving voice we internalized many years ago. This unmet yearning makes it difficult for us to open ourselves to the truth that God's love is not something we have to struggle for.

Negative Internal Messages

Part of every childhood involves balancing the signs of parental love and approval with the expressions of disappointment, disapproval, and disinterest that we

perceive. Many of us grow up convinced that we are not good enough, smart enough, important enough, athletic enough, or attractive enough to receive the love and affirmation that we need or desire. Love, even from parents, seems to have a conditional edge to it—more present when we acquiesce to the desires they have for us, or when we excel, win, and achieve than when we fail, stumble, struggle, or go our own way. Sometimes parents mete out love and approval in direct proportion to a child's success and achievement, and trying to earn parental love means pursuing an ever-receding goal.

Such unresolved personal issues block our ability to receive true unconditional love from God. We say God loves us as a father loves his own, or that God's grace sustains us as a mother embraces her children, without considering the limitations of these metaphors for people who have experienced neglect, judgment, anger, or distance from parents, or who have struggled unsuccessfully for years to earn affection.

Attitudes, Choices, Behaviors

We create our own obstacles to God's grace. We willfully deny God's gracious offer of love. By our own attitudes and behaviors we resist grace and its implications that would change us, and avoid real engagement with the interior life and its truths. We feed selfishness, self-preoccupation, and self-absorption that separate us from God and others, feverishly nurturing the resentments we harbor toward others that we do not want to let go of.

All of us have a history and have made enough destructive decisions that create large reservoirs of private shame, guilt, and regret. Desiring to follow Christ, many of us pack as if we misunderstand the purpose of the trip, bringing with us animosities, conflicts, control issues, and insecurities that weigh us down but which we find difficult to leave behind. Insistently hanging on shuts the door to God's grace and stops us from following the way of Christ.

Deep envy; unresolved jealousy; inappropriate sexual appetite; self-isolating greed; and poisonous anger, bitterness, or violence—these give us a closed posture toward God, a fear of the talk of grace and of love. We become defensive and resolute in resisting God's grace, running from God, keeping the truth from penetrating us. Clinging to life as we've come to live it, even if it feels unsatisfying or desolate, seems deceptively easier than change.

Jesus tells three stories in the fifteenth chapter of Luke that capture our disconnection from God's searching grace. The first is about Distraction. People are like sheep who distractedly nibble their way lost, mindlessly moving from one green tuft of grass to another until they are somewhere they never intended. The second is about Clutter. Why did the woman have such a difficult time finding the lost coin in her own home? Was her environment so messy, so cluttered, or so crowded that what she valued could no longer be seen without effort? She has to clean and search

to rediscover what was lost. The third is about Willful Rebellion. The prodigal son runs away from his father, consciously complicit in his own self-destructive impulses. These stories remind us that the obstacles to God's grace are not all outside ourselves, and we are not merely passive victims of negative cultural influences. Our attitudes and choices separate us from God's love and keep God's grace from penetrating our lives.

All of the distractions, clutter, and willful complicities that keep us closed to grace contribute to a dis-ease of the spirit, the atrophy of the interior life, a distance from God and God's community.

These distractions cut us off from a good life and keep us from fruitful living. These elements of distance, both inherited and willful, are what Paul describes when he says, "sin increased" (Romans 5:20). Sin is brokenness and disconnectedness from God who created us.

"ME? ASKING GOD?"

Joe Eszterhas's successful films won awards and earned him millions. But even with throat cancer destroying his larynx, he could not shake his life-long and life-threatening addictions to alcohol and tobacco. One hot sunny day, trying to outwalk fear, panic, and death, he sat down on the curb, sweating, crying, hyperventilating. He listened to himself moaning, and he heard himself mumble something. "I couldn't believe I'd said it. . . . Then I listened to myself say it again. And again and again. . . . 'Please, God, help me.' I was praying. Asking. Begging. For help. . . . And I thought to myself: 'Me? Asking God? Begging God? Praying?' I hadn't even thought about God since I was a boy. . . . And suddenly my heart was stilled. . . . I stopped trembling and twitching." As he rose to return home, he realized he was not alone, "I thought I could do it now. . . . It would be excruciatingly difficult, but with God's help, I thought I could do it." Eszterhas doesn't know whether to describe his experienced as God finding him or him finding God. That day he accepted God's acceptance of himself. It was a day of grace.[5]

Is there a way out, or a way through the obstacles, to the life God intends for us? How can we live fruitfully, happily, and meaningfully in the face of these recurring obstacles that separate us from God?

Opening to Grace

Beneath the daily surface life, there continually streams a spiritual dimension, an interior life, a richly sacred and eternal depth. In unexpected moments, events press us deeper than the superficial and invite us to search for answers to questions we haven't even thought to ask before. These moments mark the intersection of daily life and the life of the spirit, the interweaving of the mundane with the sacred, the intermingling of the immediate practical questions of getting along with the deeper questions of direction and purpose. In these moments of intrusion, events jar us into encounter with the deeper mysteries, and we may perceive God's grace reaching out to us.

Some of those moments include the birth of a child; when our children leave home for college, military service, or work; a serious health threat or accident; the death of a family member or close friend; a national tragedy or natural disaster; a painful reversal at work or an unanticipated success; the start or end of a new relationship. In all of these, we find ourselves exploring the question of what lasts.

Such events interrupt our surface existence with penetrating and life-changing impact. They cause us to face questions that the tangibles of a materialist culture or the certainties of reason do nothing to help us understand. We yearn for answers that cannot be provided by how much money we have, what kind of car we drive, or what newest celebrity gossip we know. Tangible, transient, and surface satisfactions cannot imbue our lives with the meaning we thirst for. These moments of reflection represent the intrusion into our lives of eternity and its questions, the gentle tapping on our shoulder of angels, the whispers of the Spirit. These moments create openings, make us aware of our yearning, and place us in a posture of curiosity and desire. They make us willing to open the door to God's love and ready to receive what God's grace may mean for our lives.

What's the purpose and end for which we were created? What is trustworthy and true? Who am I? How does God fit in to it all?

The answers do not come from outside of us. We never earn enough, do enough, or achieve enough to guarantee happiness. We do not become what God created us to be simply by more activity, faster motion, working harder, or having more stuff. More intensity on these external activities does not satisfy the soul.

And contrary to self-help books, the good life cannot come from inside us by our own efforts either. We do not achieve it by trying harder, pushing further, pulling ourselves up

by our own bootstraps. Self-love, self-absorption, and self-focus do not take us there.

Happiness, meaning, and contribution come from connection to the source of life, from the grace we've become accustomed to closing out and denying by our distraction, clutter, and complicity. The door we've been closing on God's grace has been shutting us off from what we need the most.

The good life comes from the practice of hospitality toward God, opening ourselves to God, and making room in our hearts for the gift-like transformation God's love makes possible. Happiness results from patterns of living that draw us closer to God and one another, from practices that open and reopen the connections that bind us to God and to the community. We flourish as we learn to love and be loved, and to serve and be served. Flourishing comes from the sheer volume of human relationships that grace our lives; fruitful living results from an outward focus,

from demonstrably loving others through the offering of ourselves to make a difference. Love changes everything.

Hospitality toward God opens us to new life. In the practice of making space for God in our hearts again and again, we accept God's gift of new life.

Mitch

Mitch grew up with no faith background. His alcoholic father was arrested for stealing money and was discovered having an extramarital affair, causing Mitch to have to change schools as a consequence of his parents' divorce. Mitch lost his friends, the job he loved, and his place on the baseball team. He developed a violent temperament, ran with rough characters, and made his own way in a tough world of sports, drinking, and hard living. During his early twenties, he lived with a seething anger toward his father that moved through his soul like a slow-moving river. His envy toward others ate at him, for the advantages they

had received that he had been denied. He was angry about things that would never be resolved.

Mitch developed a tough veneer that hid any deeper sense of compassion. He had no faith, no church, no God, and no positive models for how to handle his life. He worked as a truck driver until he saved enough money to pay his way through college. He flirted with drug and alcohol abuse, but by sheer personal determination, he didn't get pulled irretrievably into these habits.Mitch met a young woman who was committed to her faith. In preparation for their marriage, he had several conversations with her pastor. He came to respect the pastor, to learn from him, and to look forward to their times together. When Mitch married, he decided that he would "try church." "Is this for real?" was the inner question he wrestled with during his early hesitating steps toward faith. For months he attended with his wife, finding the worship service a confusing litany of language and images and prayers. He felt like an outsider, but he was determined to make it work. He and his wife

connected with a Sunday school class for young couples. Mitch was invited to help at a community soup kitchen that serves the homeless, and he accepted. He was invited to help with the finance committee, and then with the trustees. He found these strangely satisfying, but he continued to feel turned off by small-minded attitudes and cliquishness. Mitch began to read the Bible, to experiment with praying, to volunteer a little more here and there. He helped with the youth ministry, especially the sports and outdoor activities. He particularly offered himself to work with the difficult kids.

Mitch experienced a deepening of his faith through the weekend adult retreat called *Walk to Emmaus*. He committed to the in-depth DISCIPLE Bible study, and eventually became a Bible study teacher himself, especially effective at gathering younger men who had never had any experience in studying Scripture. He offered himself as a team leader for hands-on service projects to build and repair homes for people in poverty. Through his nonjudgmental approach

toward people, he became instrumental in helping many unchurched people get involved in various ministries.

Mitch's language is still rough, his manner brusque, and his approach to church and tolerance for protocol are, shall we say, less traditional. He relates well to professionals, feels like one of the boys among hardworking folk—oil riggers, ranch hands, and construction crews. When someone is going through a difficult time, he gives them his phone number and tells them to call him anytime, anywhere, and he'll come. Mitch believes the church really does change lives.

By the grace of God, Mitch has become someone different from the life that was scripted for him. Through faith in Christ, formed and cultivated through fifteen years of worship, learning, and service, Mitch has found the power to avoid the destructive impulses that undid his father and derailed his family of origin. By the practice of daily submitting himself to Christ, Mitch has come to a

place he could never imagine—a sense of satisfaction and contribution, of making a difference and doing good in the lives of others.

The Apostle Paul writes, "So if anyone is in Christ, there is a new creation: everything old has passed away; see, everything has become new!" (2 Corinthians 5:17).

Mitch is a new creation. Over time, he has arrived at a place he never would have come to on his own. He is a radically different person from what he would have been had he never walked the path of faith in Christ.

Look back over Mitch's story and notice the many signs of receptivity, moments when he could have said *No*, but instead said *Yes* on the spiritual journey. Agreeing to meet with the pastor and to attend church with his wife, overcoming the awkwardness of worship, attending a young couples class, volunteering to help with the soup kitchen, initiating Bible study, experimenting with prayer— each of these became a stepping-stone, a building block

toward growth in Christ. Each was a sign of his hospitality toward God and of a willingness to allow God to enter in. At each key point, he received God, opened himself to the spiritual life, and welcomed God to play a larger role in his life. Following Christ has been a continuing lifelong process of opening his heart to God.

REFLECTION

Now we look inside,
and what we see is that anyone
UNITED *with the* MESSIAH
gets a FRESH START,
is created NEW.
The old life is gone;
A NEW LIFE BURGEONS!
LOOK AT IT!

—*2 Corinthians 5:17 , The Message*

Happiness, meaning, and
contribution come from
connection to the source of life

Questions

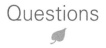

• What obstacles do you strive to overcome in order to fully receive God's love?

• What makes it difficult for you to open yourself to the truth of God's love for you? What distracts you from the spiritual life or clutters the way to God for you?

• What unexpected moments or situations have brought you to a new or deeper receptivity to God and God's grace?

Prayer

Give me a fresh start; create me new. You are the potter, Lord, and I am the clay. Mold me to your purpose. Make me your own.

Receiving God's Love

THE PRACTICE OF RADICAL HOSPITALITY:
Inviting God into Our Lives and
Making Room for God in Our Hearts

> *For by grace you have been saved*
> *through faith, and this is not your*
> *own doing; it is a gift of God.*
> *—Ephesians 2:8*

The personal practice of Radical Hospitality begins with accepting God's love for us offered through Christ and deciding to let that gracious love make a difference in our lives. It's an attitude; a mind-set; an openness to spiritual things; a willingness to listen, perceive, and receive God's presence and initiative. The decision to receive God marks the start of our own journey and soul work, the first step toward a dynamic and vibrant life with God. It involves the critical decision, "Will I open the door to the spiritual life or leave it closed? Will I listen for God, invite God into my heart and allow God's grace to shape my life, or not?" This receptivity expresses a willingness, a submission, a yearning. It involves a desire to put ourselves into God's hands, to being shaped into something new that we cannot now see. When we adopt this attitude of acceptance, and say *Yes* to God's initiating grace, we begin down a path that is presently unknown to us and that only becomes knowable as time unfolds. We say *Yes* to being a disciple, a learner, and follower, trusting that as surely as others have been changed and shaped by this critical decision, so shall we.

RECEPTIVITY

Mary Ann describes spiritual receptivity this way: "You clear a space for the Spirit's voice, and close the door to as many other voices as possible—things to be done, people to meet, anxiety, guilt, duty. These are always pushing. You slide closed the door for a few moments. Listening for God takes persistence. The still, small voice is hard to recognize. But if you sit there long enough, something will happen. Peace, a letting go, a centering. An opening. If I practice it every day, I get better at it."

The personal practice of Radical Hospitality continues and is sustained with deliberate behaviors, the pursuing of a deepening relationship with God through practices that place us in the most advantageous position to continue to welcome Christ, and make room for grace.

Radical Hospitality toward God involves both the attitude of receptivity and intentional practice.

We intuitively know that connection, meaning, and contribution come from cultivating the interior life, the spiritual life, life with God. Something inside wants to be healed and to become whole. Something within knows that there is more than the surface existence. There is an inner wanting and waiting beyond conscious awareness, a curiosity, a ripeness and readiness to receive. God's grace (prevenient grace, as Wesley calls it, that makes ready our responses to God's offering of love before we even realize it) prepares us to accept that we are accepted, to say *Yes*, and to begin the journey.

OPEN THE DOOR

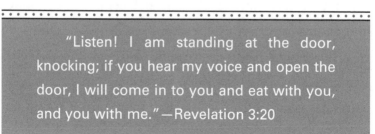

"Listen! I am standing at the door, knocking; if you hear my voice and open the door, I will come in to you and eat with you, and you with me." —Revelation 3:20

People who cultivate receptivity look for ways to invite God in rather than to close God out; they deliberately seek to say *Yes* to the promptings of the Spirit rather than to deny or avoid them.

They regularly ask for God's help, simply, humbly, and in no special language but their own. They desire God's presence.

They make space in their lives, room in their hearts, and time in their schedules to focus on interior work. Nurturing the spirit becomes as essential as feeding the body; soul work becomes as important as physical exercise. They open hearts and minds to God.

They invite interruptions by God into their lives, interventions of the Spirit, unexpected opportunities for doing what is life-giving.

They look for sightings of the Spirit's work, evidence of God prompting love, service, generosity, sacrifice. They learn to perceive God.

People who demonstrate the quality of hospitality toward God are curious about God, spirituality, and the interior life. They desire to know God rather than merely to know about God.

Those who practice receptivity to God enjoy the exploration of the spiritual life and embrace following Jesus as an adventure. They delight in new learning. They do not view religion as a burden, a mere duty, or as something that weighs heavy. Spirituality lifts them up.

The word *radical* intensifies the notion of receptivity. *Radical* means "outside the norm, drastically different from ordinary practice," and so it connotes giving priority and intentionality to receiving God into our lives. *Radical* derives from the word "root" and describes a profound, deep-rooted receptivity. Those who practice *Radical Hospitality* invite God into the core of their existence; seeking God becomes a fundamental and defining element of their existence.

Many of us approach the spiritual life the way we would an interesting hobby or constructive pastime, like fishing, gardening, golfing, or belonging to a book club. Being Christian comprises a small part of our identity. We attend church when it's convenient, we pick up some helpful insights and enjoy the people, and we serve on committees to help the organization run smoothly. Church, religion, and the spiritual life provide some benefit, but we remain puzzlingly remote from real interior work, mystery, or notions of grace. Practicing religion in this way *confirms* something about ourselves rather than *transforming* the nature of who we are. Religion is not really a power for living; it is an appendage to an otherwise harried and hectic schedule. Religion is more about attending church than following Christ. For many of us, personal prayer is incidental to the flow of life; serving others is something we do to be a faithful part of the team; contributing money involves doing our fair share. It's not that we close the door on God, we just haven't made much effort to seriously receive God fully into our lives.

Those people we admire because they display a depth, passion, integrity, and wisdom forged by a dynamic and vibrant faith have not taken the spiritual life so casually. At some fundamental point, they decided to receive God, to offer a hospitality that goes the second mile—an uncommon, radical hospitality toward God. Instead of going to visit God for an hour each week they bring God home with them, giving God place, priority, devotion. They explore the interior life. They reach for God and open themselves to God's reaching for them. They internalize faith for themselves, a faith that isn't perfunctory or empty, but which is a dynamic force in their lives. They open themselves to God in a radical way. They have said *Yes*, and *Yes* again, and they are immensely richer for doing so.

Even with many years of church experience, many of us may find ourselves still standing on the front porch of the life that is possible in Christ because we've never fully entered in. Or to change the metaphor, we may have left God standing on the front porch of our lives without fully

receiving him. We've left undiscovered the "immeasurable riches of God's grace," "abundant life," and "a peace that surpasses all understanding."

People who practice Radical Hospitality toward God move beyond a tentative willingness to sample faith; they actively demonstrate an intentional receptivity to God. They make critical decisions because of their relationship with God. They allow God to become a principal part of their life and they become part of God's life. They lay open their hearts.

They *want* God to change them, to make them anew. A God-related life becomes an important stabilizing and orienting force. Growing in Christ becomes an objective.

People who practice receptivity realize that the spiritual journey requires deliberate, continuing cooperation with God. They practice, repeat, and deepen the core essentials that open themselves to God. The Christian life is more than knowledge about Jesus; it is a lifestyle to be mastered.

Receptivity means that the question, "Am I pleased with my life?" is matched and balanced with the question, "Is my life pleasing to God?" Rather than seeking something from God, they seek God.

They realize that deepening the spirit does not come quickly, that following Jesus can be inconvenient, and that gradually surrendering control to God is uncomfortable. They don't cling to the fantasy that spiritual maturity, satisfaction, and contribution fall into place easily. Saying *Yes* to grace empowers them and strengthens them to say *No* to many other things.

People who practice Radical Hospitality realize that opening themselves to God also involves opening themselves to the community of faith.

They are resilient and persistent, and they are not afraid to wrestle with God. Even when they are more keenly aware of God's absence than of God's presence, they persevere in the trust that in their searching, they are found.

They live with a less anxious attitude. In opening themselves to God's grace, they receive their validation. They are loved once, finally, and forever by God in Christ. By accepting God's love for them, nothing remains conditional, ambiguous, or incomplete about their ultimate worth. They build their house upon a rock.

They strive to love the things God loves, to want the things God wants, to find happiness in the things God gives, to find meaning in God's work. They seek first God's kingdom, and all else follows from that.

Accept that you are accepted. The first step toward fruitful living involves saying *Yes* to God's unconditional love toward us. God's love changes everything. The opening of ourselves to God's grace stimulates a passionate desire to love God in return, and this takes us to the second practice of fruitful living, Passionate Worship.

REFLECTION

We LOVE *because* HE *first* LOVED US.

—*1 John 4:19*

Accept that you are accepted. The first step toward fruitful living involves saying Yes to God's unconditional love toward us. God's love changes everything.

Questions

- How do your present patterns of living invite God in or cause you to avoid the spiritual life?

- When did you last evaluate your relationship with God? How are you closed to God's grace, and how are you open?

- What steps can you take to reshape your life toward greater receptivity?

- How do you plan to say *Yes* to God's grace today? Everyday?

Prayer

God, help me love the things you love and want the things you want. Get me walking in your way. Open my heart to love the people you have placed in my life.

Leader Helps
for Small Group Sessions

Receiving God's Love

Focus Point: Radical Hospitality involves being receptive to God's love and intentionally making room for God in our lives.

GETTING READY *(Prior to the Session)*

Preparation:
• Read Chapter 1 in Receiving God's Love.
• Write the key Scripture and focus points on a board or chart.
• Review Digging In and Making Application, and select the points and discussion questions you will cover.
• Acquire a box of index cards and a bag of pens.
• Pray for the session and for your group members.

Key Scripture: *"We love because he first loved us." 1 John 4:19*

Main Ideas:
• The first step in our walk of faith is saying Yes to God's unconditional love for us. Faith is our acceptance of God's gift of grace. We receive God's grace, love, and pardon, and allow these gifts to shape us and make us anew.

GETTING STARTED

Opening Prayer
Gracious God, you love us unconditionally and accept us unreservedly. All we have to do is open ourselves to your love and accept your gift. Teach us to cultivate the practice of Radical Hospitality in our lives, of opening ourselves again and again to you and making a place in our hearts for your love. In Jesus' name we pray. Amen.

DIGGING IN

Direct participants to p. 19. Have someone read the first paragraph aloud. *[The personal practice of radical hospitality begins with…]*
Now have participants find the statement, "You are loved. You are loved. You are loved. Can you accept that?"

Group Discussion
• How have you felt/experienced God's unconditional love?
• Have you truly accepted that you are loved and accepted by God? If not, what is keeping you from accepting this reality?
• Have you ever felt that you must strive for, earn, or fear God's love? Why?

The Practice of Radical Hospitality

Briefly present Tillich's concept of being "struck by grace." Emphasize the following points:
• When God's grace strikes us, we are faced with the startling reality of God's unconditional love for us.
• This realization jars us into a new way of thinking.
• Receiving and understanding the love and forgiveness of God opens us to new life, and this can be as abrupt as lightening and as disruptive as an earthquake.

Group Discussion
• What do you understand the phrase "struck by grace" to mean?
• How have you been struck by God's grace?

MAKING APPLICATION

What Does It Look Like?
Have participants turn to John Wesley's story. Be prepared to summarize the story, noting the highlights.

Briefly Discuss
• When have you felt your heart strangely warmed with the assurance of God's love for you?

Read aloud the passage from Chapter 1 in Receiving God's Love beginning with, "The piercing quality of God's love disrupts people (p.35)."

Hand out note cards and pens to each participant. Ask them to write the following questions along with their answers on their note cards. These answers will not be shared, but encourage them to keep this card in their Bibles or books and bring them each week as they will add to the list.
• What would greater receptivity or openness to God look like for my life?
• Thinking about the next 3–5 years, what patterns do I hope God will use to reshape my life? How will I begin these patterns/practices?

What Now?
Instruct participants to reflect silently in response to this question:
• In light of all we have shared today, what do you sense God saying to you?

End by inviting answers to these questions:
• In response, what will you do differently this week?
• How will what you learned this week change how you live your life?

Close your session with prayer requests and invite a participant to close in prayer.

Receiving God's Love

Focus Point: Many obstacles prevent us from receiving God's love making us inhospitable to God's initiative including cultural voices and fast-forward living.

GETTING READY *(Prior to the Session)*

Preparation:
• Read Chapter 2 in Receiving God's Love.
• Write the key Scripture and focus points on a board or chart.
• Review Digging In and Making Application, and select the points and discussion questions you will cover.
• Pray for the session and for your group members.

Key Scripture: *"Do not be conformed to this world, but be transformed by the renewing of your minds, so that you may discern what is the will of God—what is good and acceptable and perfect." Romans 12:2*

Main Ideas:
• The voices of our commercial culture influence us through television, radio, magazines, and the Internet; and all these voices influence our perceptions of ourselves.
• The notion of a life abundant and fruitful, comes from deeper sources. It grows from the awareness that God loves us.
• God is in the depth, and we lose touch with God when we focus only on surface things.
• Hearing God requires deliberate soul work. Spirituality and speed do not go together well.

GETTING STARTED

Opening Prayer
Gracious God, you love us in the deepest parts of our hearts, the ones we try to hide or busy ourselves to forget. You call us to slow down, to listen, to go deeper. Teach us to cultivate the practice of Radical Hospitality, of opening ourselves again and again to you and making a place in our hearts for your love. In Jesus' name we pray. Amen.

DIGGING IN

Have someone read the first two paragraphs of this chapter.

Now direct the group to the second passage that begins with, "The voices of our commercial culture repeat themselves over and over . . . " (p. 40).

Group Discussion
• What are some of the cultural voices and pressures that keep us from a deeper spiritual life?
• Why is it so easy to fill up our lives with things other than intentional spiritual formation?
• When was the last time you really felt at peace?

Briefly summarize the concept of "Fast-Forward Living" (p. 42).

Group Discussion
- How often would you say you stop and consider the depth of your life with God?
- What kinds of things drain our energy without having earned a place of high priority in our lives?
- What does it take to change this pattern?

Ask someone to read aloud "It Fits Me Better" (p. 46).

Group Discussion
- When have you had a moment of awareness and made an immediate decision to change course?

MAKING APPLICATION

What Does It Look Like?
- Have participants turn to p. 49. Invite a volunteer to read aloud the paragraph that begins, "Today it's hard to develop…".

Briefly Discuss:
- Why do you think spirituality and speed do not go together well?

Read aloud the passage that begins, *"Fifty or sixty years of a life defined by doing what's next . . ." (p. 50).*

Ask participants to pull out their note cards from last week. Invite them to write two new questions along with their answers on their note cards. These answers will not be shared, but encourage them to keep this card in their Bibles or books and bring them each week as they will add to the list.

- What obstacles or distractions keep you from fully receiving God's love?
- How do your present patterns of living invite God in or cause you to avoid the spiritual life?

What Now?
Instruct participants to reflect silently in response to this question:
- In light of all we have shared today, what do you sense God saying to you?

End by inviting answers to these questions:
- In response, what will you do differently this week?
- How will what you learned this week change how you live your life?

Close your session with prayer requests and invite a participant to close in prayer.

Receiving God's Love

SESSION 3: *Obstacles to Grace—Internal Messages and Personal Choices*

Focus Point: The good life comes from patterns of opening ourselves to God's grace rather than closing ourselves off from God.

GETTING READY *(Prior to the Session)*

Preparation:
• Read Chapter 3 in Receiving God's Love.
• Write the key Scripture and focus points on a board or chart.
• Review Digging In and Making Application, and select the points and discussion questions you will cover.
• Pray for the session and for your group members.

Key Scripture: "*So if anyone is in Christ, there is a new creation: everything old has passed away; see, everything has become new!*" 2 Corinthians 5:17

Main Ideas:
• In addition to external distractions, internal pressures also complicate receiving God's love.
• By our own attitudes and behaviors we resist grace and its implications that would change us, and avoid real engagement with the interior life and its truths.
• The good life comes from the practice of hospitality toward God, opening ourselves to God, and making room in our hearts for the gift-like transformation God's love makes possible.

GETTING STARTED

Opening Prayer

Gracious God, your grace waits for us even when we've avoided it for years. Sometimes the baggage we carry and our internal dialogue are like a barricade between our hearts and your love. Help us drop our baggage, change the soundtrack in our minds, and run to you. . In Jesus' name we pray. Amen.

DIGGING IN

Direct participants to find Chapter 3. Read aloud the excerpt that begins, "The answers do not come from outside of us" (p. 62).

Briefly review the things mentioned that result in the happiness found in "the good life": patterns of living that draw us closer to God.

Group Discussion
• Compare the inner happiness that comes from God's Spirit with the happiness defined by culture.
• What personal patterns and practices help you to cultivate the good life?

Point out that sometimes we are not receptive to God's grace until unexpected situations or experiences break into our interior lives, causing us to ask questions and making us aware of our yearning.

Group Discussion
• What unexpected moments or situations have brought you to a new or deeper receptivity to God and God's grace?

MAKING APPLICATION *(15–20 minutes)*

What Does It Look Like?
• Have participants turn to Mitch's story (p. 64).
Briefly Discuss
• What signs of receptivity can you identify in Mitch's story—moments when he could have said No but instead said Yes to God?
• What are the obstacles?

Acknowledge that there are many obstacles that prevent us from receiving God's love and make us inhospitable to God's initiative as we've seen in Chapters 2 and 3. Ask the group to name the ones they found true in their own lives.

Invite participants to pull out their note cards from last week. Ask them to write two new questions along with their answers on their note cards. These answers will not be shared, but encourage them to keep this card in their Bibles or books and bring them each week as they will add to the list.

• What personal choices do you need to make to become more receptive to God's Spirit?
• What can you do to change the inner narrative from anxiousness, anger, or guilt to peace, joy, and hope?

What Now?
Reflect silently together on: In light of all we have shared today, what do you sense God saying to you?

End by inviting answers to these questions:
• In response, what will you do differently this week?
• How will what you learned this week change how you live your life?

Close your session with prayer requests and invite a participant to close in prayer.

Receiving God's Love

The Practice of Radical Hospitality—Inviting God into Our Lives and Making Room for God in Our Hearts

Focus Point: The personal practice of Radical Hospitality begins with accepting God's love for us offered through Christ, and deciding to let that gracious love make a difference in our lives.

GETTING READY *(Prior to the Session)*

Preparation:
• Read Chapter 4 in Receiving God's Love.
• Write the key Scripture and focus points on a board or chart.
• Review Digging In and Making Application, and select the points and discussion questions you will cover.
• Pray for the session and for your group members.

Key Scripture: *For by grace you have been saved through faith, and this is not your own doing; it is a gift of God. Ephesians 2:8*

Main Ideas:
• The personal practice of Radical Hospitality begins with accepting God's love for us offered through Christ, and deciding to let that gracious love make a difference in our lives.
• Radical Hospitality toward God involves both receptivity and intentional practice.
• People who cultivate receptivity look for ways to invite God in rather than to close God out.
• The first step toward fruitful living involves saying Yes to God's unconditional love toward us. God's love changes everything.

GETTING STARTED

Opening Prayer
Gracious God, your love astounds us. We don't get it, but we need it. Help us to make room for you in our lives. Let your love change our lives. In Jesus' name we pray. Amen.

DIGGING IN

Read aloud the passage from the chapter that begins, "The personal practice of Radical Hospitality begins with accepting God's love for us offered through Christ . . ." (p. 74).

Briefly review Mary Ann's experience in the paragraph titled, Receptivity.

Group Discussion
• Why does Radical Hospitality begin with accepting God's love?
• What is required of us in order for God to change us?

Read or summarize the paragraph that begins, "Many of us approach the spiritual life the way we would an interesting hobby or constructive pastime . . ." (p. 79).

Group Discussion
- What is your initial response to this paragraph? Where does your response come from, do you think?
- What is the distinction between attending church and following Christ?
- What would your life look like if you received God fully into your life?

MAKING APPLICATION

What Does It Look Like?
Direct participants to the section beginning, "People who cultivate receptivity look for ways . . ." (p. 77). Point out that Radical Hospitality involves receptivity and intentional practice. Then highlight some of the habits of people who practice Radical Hospitality from the rest of Chapter 4. Encourage participants to underline these habits in their chapters as they see them.

Briefly discuss
- Which habits listed do you most need to put some effort into?

Invite participants to pull out their note cards from last week. Ask them to write two new questions along with their answers on their note cards.
- When did you last evaluate your relationship with God? How are you closed to God's grace, and how are you open?
- What steps can you take to reshape your life toward greater receptivity?

What Now?
Instruct participants to reflect silently in response to this question:
- In light of all we have shared today, what do you sense God saying to you?

End by inviting answers to these questions:
- In response to these sessions on Radical Hospitality, what will you do differently this week?
- How will what you learned this week and in the book Radical Hospitality change how you live your life?

Close your session with prayer requests and invite a participant to close in prayer.

Notes

1 All Tillich quotes and references in this chapter are from his sermon, "You Are Accepted," contained in Paul Tillich's The Shaking of the Foundations (Charles Scribner's Sons, 1948); pp. 161–162.

2 Anne Lamott, Traveling Mercies (Anchor Books, 1999); p. 141.

3 John Wesley, Works, Vol. 1, "Journal From Oct. 14, 1735, to Feb. 1, 1737-8"; p. 103.

4 For further discussion of this paradox and the trends and sources of happiness, see Dick Meyer's book Why We Hate Us: American Discontent in the New Millennium (Three Rivers Press, 2009).

5 Joe Eszterhas, Crossbearer (St. Martin's Press, 2008); pp. 3–5.